GIANT TARANTULAS AND CENIPEDES

NORTHWATER

CONSTANTINE ISSIGHOS

Copyright 2013 © Constantine Issighos. Published in Canada. Printed in U.S.A. No part of this book may be reproduced or transmitted in any form or by any means, electronic or mechanical, including photocopying, recording, and/or by any information storage and retrieval system except by a reviewer who may quote brief passages in a review to be printed in a magazine, newspaper, or on the web without written permission in writing from the author/publisher. For information, please contact www.awaqkunabooks.com

NorthWater is an imprint of Awaqkuna Books Inc.

Vol. 19 Of THE AMAZON EXPLORATION SERIES:
GIANT TARANTULAS AND CENTIPES

Library and Archives Canada

ISBN ISBN 978-0-9878601-8-7

Library and Archives Canada Cataloguing in Publication

ATTENTION CHILDRENS ASSOCIATIONS, BOOK STORES, PUBLIC OR PRIVATE LIBRARIES: quantity discounts are available on bulk purchases of this book series.

THE AMAZON EXPLORATION SERIES
Children's Books
by
Constantine Issighos

1. Upper Amazon Voyage by River Boat
2. The People of the River
3. The Children of the River
4. Amazon's Nature of Things
5. Echoes of Nature: a Beautiful Wild Habitat
6. The Amazon Rainforest
7. Amazonian Sisterhood
8. Amazon River Wolves
9. Amazonian Landscapes and Sunsets
10. Amazonian Canopy: the Roof of the World's Rainforest
11. Amazonian Tribes: a World of Difference
12. Birds and Butterflies of the Amazon
13. The Great Wonders of the Amazon
14. The Jaguar People
15. The Fresh Water Giants
16. The Call of the Shamans
17. Indigenous Families: Life in Harmony with Nature
18. Amazon in Peril
19. Giant Tarantulas and Centipes
20. Amazon Ethnobotanical Garden
21. Amazon Tribal Warrios

Everything that I read had warned me – be ready for a blast of heat and humidity upon stepping out of a plane in the Amazon. It was Feb. the hottest month of the year. I had taken the 35 minute flight from Piura, Peru to the jungle city of Iquitos. I landed at the airport to find myself in the humid Amazon basin for the first time in my life. A 2 hour bus ride to the town of Nauta gave me a good indication of the movements and noises of the local people. As soon as the bus stopped, passengers were surrounded by persistent taxi and boat drivers, as well as vendors selling locally-produced fruits, candy, banana chips, oranges, Brazil nuts and star fruit juice. What a commotion!

My purpose for visiting the Province of Loreto was to experience first-hand all that I had heard about the jungle of the Upper Amazon. I also wanted to confirm whether this trip would lead me to write a series books about life in the Amazon rainforest.

My guide Marco and I were up early the next morning for a dugout canoe trip to a village not too far from Nauta. The village was made up of a series of wooden huts, each constructed of local material, with poles and palm leaves for the roof. Each hut was 3 meters (12 feet) in height with a 2-slope roof, and was divided in to a series of partitions for sleeping, cooking bathroom etc. The huts were joined by communal wooden walkways which served as protection from flooding and insects.

For the foreign visitors' convenience, there was a net covering the height of each window to keep out uninvited jungle life of the creeping and crawling variety such as bats, giant cockroaches, spiders, tarantulas and centipedes. My bed was covered with an industrial strength mosquito net that kept out everything, including air! All these measures, however, did not prevent these creeping bugs from finding their way in and sharing my accommodations.

High on the ceiling were the tarantulas, wolf spiders, centipedes, giant cockroaches and many other things that I was not particularly interested in getting acquainted with. I was lucky to have a private bathroom—well, just me, the tarantulas and the centipedes.

While staying in the village, I boarded long motorized canoes at various times of the day and night to conduct visual surveys of the land and river animal life. Along these physically demanding trails in the thick rainforest, machete-wielding path-opening was often the only way to proceed. Arrival was an approximation, not an exact destination in this area where it is rare to see the Red-Uakari monkeys; a species that inhabits only this area of the Peruvian Amazon.

During my journey into this remote area of the jungle, I developed many fond memories which solidified my decision to return to the Amazon rainforest to photograph and write about its wildlife. I have to admit that I have not so many fond memories of the jungle's large population of leaf- cutter ants, chiggers, mosquitoes, pink-toe tarantulas, palm spiders and giant centipedes. They seemed to be everywhere with their incredible ability to crawl onto my hammock and into my traveling bags and our supplies. As night fell, the various populations of bats emerged, along with the giant insects, followed by the owls who also hunted the insects for their evening meal.

My guide Marco reminded me to avoid fastening my hammock onto any tree occupied by leaf cutter ants. The leaf-cutter ants (Atta sexdens) feed on fresh leaves, fruits, flowers, tubers and the stems of plants. Leaf-cutters travel long distances from their nests in order to find new and better foliage. The ants move in single file, devouring everything on their way, often leaving visible trails through tree bark or the forest floor. Some indigenous tribes find the leaf-cutters a good source of protein and others use its jaws as stitches to hold together the edges of a wound.

Early the next morning, I decided to return to Nauta and plan my next guided exploration. Well! It is not often that a pink-toe tarantula seeks to make my acquaintance! One did just that when it casually hopped off one of my bags on board our motorized canoe as we began to pull away from the riverbank. Marcos instructed me to calmly let "Pink-Toes" parade along my arm. I did just that, as I simultaneously zoomed my camera on our beguiling hitchhiker. "Don't be afraid" Marcos said with a mile-wide grin, "The tarantula won't hurt you unless it feels threatened." I passed the tarantula among us for a stroll on our caps, arms and vests.

"Pink-Toes" is just one of the many unexpected surprises that I encountered which helped me make my final decision to return (someday!) to write about the Amazon Basin. I thought that if a supersized bug, jewel-like birds, and one giant anaconda on the river enticed me for an adventure, then the Upper Amazon was for me.

During my brief visits to various sites, my curiosity served to focus my direction. Each species of aquatic and land animal, each tribal village or settlement and each unexpected landscape became one more story to be told.

Upon returning to Nauta, I asked my guide Marcos about the people in the area who are doing their best to preserve the ecosystem and endangered animals. He replied that there is a group of young conservationists who gather wounded animals for treatment and possible release back into the wild. I told Marcos that I wanted to stay away from tourist traps. He assured me that the animal sanctuary on the Isla de los Monos (Island of the Monkeys) was not one of them.

During the motorized canoe ride it was easy to spot beautiful bright birds, such as herons and kingfishers, amongst the scattered native huts. Upon arrival at the Isla de los Monos Sanctuary, I decided to take a walk along the raised boardwalks through the dense flooded palm forest where the sanctuary's animals are often sighted.

The animal sanctuary on the Isla de los Monos consists of a few wooden structures which serve as huts for the volunteers who work there. There are trails that lead further on from the sanctuary's main clearing. Other marked trails lead towards some huts that were occupied by about a dozen European female college students.

At the sanctuary gate, there was a pair of colourful parrots who seemed to have adopted the entryway, guarding it by sounding warning screeches at anyone who approached it, including the staff. Within the sanctuary I found many species of avocado, rows of banana plants with recovering baby monkeys playing on the branches, prehistoric freshwater turtles, boas, tapirs, sloths and a number of centipedes and tarantulas.

By this time I was accustomed to seeing moving centipedes and tarantulas on posts, ceilings and houseplants. What I was not accustomed to was finding a number of tarantulas lying dead on the forest floor or hanging dead on a plant's branches. They appeared to be intact, without any missing parts on their notable legs or on their main body. When I lifted one up, however, I noticed that it was hollow and very light in weight.

I showed one dead tarantula to a staff member who pointed out a number of "evil-looking" tarantula-wasps. It was explained to me that they were "evil" wasps because they sting the tarantulas and inject their eggs inside them. When the eggs hatch, the larvae start to eat the tarantula alive from the inside, killing it slowly. Creepy things!

Evening was fast approaching, so I decided to spend the night in the sanctuary. My guide Marcos and I went for a night walk armed with just our torches. I wanted to see more live tarantula spiders. We were quite literally just a few yards away from our hut when I was asked to switch off my torch. Marcos crept quietly ahead to have a look around in the undergrowth and then beckoned me to approach quietly—in the dark! When I had come close to him, Marcos shone his torch on a group of large tarantula spiders. Needless to say, the tarantulas did not like the sudden attention and crawled away into their burrows.

However, a group of female student visitors got a little more excited by the proximity of a few 9cm (4' inches) tarantula spiders in the sanctuary's communal showers. The shower walls did not quite reach the floor and I could see the occupant's ankles. I am convinced that some of the students probably thought that they did not really need a fresh shower on this humid night! We continued our night walk further into the jungle. I saw a large armour-plated centipede, a large scorpion-spider and plenty of fire-ants, which I was very careful not to step on them as they were everywhere. That night, I went to bed and slept very fitfully considering the potential for nocturnal visitors.

The following morning I visited the aquatic facility where the sanctuary's ill manatees were being cared for. This facility is run by young volunteer conservationists with backgrounds in biology. They explained to me that many of the manatees suffer from boat propeller wounds, particularly the baby manatees, who seem to go unnoticed by passing motorized canoe drivers. Here the staff is very conscientious about the level of each manatee's injuries. Depending on the type of injuries, some of these gentle aquatic animals are treated for more than a year, others for less time. Once they are returned to health, the manatees are slowly re-introduced back into the wild.

While there, I heard a commotion in another part of the facility. One of the staff brought in Oskar, the sanctuary's dog, who seemed to be ill. It appeared that the dog had chosen the wrong playmate, the bird-eater spider, to have fun with, and it was bitten.

Despite its name, this tarantula rarely eats birds. Spanning cm17 (7" inches) with its legs and weighing nearly 125 grams (¼ of a lb) this tarantula is the largest spider in the world. It hunts large prey, but not bigger than itself, including insects, lizards and frogs. During the rainy season, this tarantula migrates into the trees where it ambushes and grabs its prey.

People of the Amazon find this tarantula to be high in proteins; they double-in its legs and roast it over an open campfire. Of course, people have to be careful when they handle bird-eater tarantulas since they can deliver a painful, but non-lethal, venomous bite. The tarantulas have irritating abnormal hair that they can flick at the eyes and skin of attackers causing them to itch. In the case of Oskar his reactions could have been more serious had it not been for the staffs' quick medical response. In a few days Oskar would recover back to his normal playful self.

My preliminary exploration for future themes would not have been complete without writing something about the people of the Amazon rainforest.

The Upper Amazon region was discovered and conquered by Spanish explorers in 1541, followed by a number of generations of settlers who form part of today's human legacy. People with Spanish ancestors who live along the rivers and tributaries are called "ribernos" or "metizos." They live in small villages or settlements, cultivate small plots, fish and hunt. They talk with a Spanish accent (distinct from a Latino accent) and have dark skin and hair. They wear similar clothing to people in the western world. They maintain a very simple life, grow fruits and vegetables in small gardens and trade in the city for manufactured goods.

People whose ancestors lived for thousands of years in the Amazon rainforest are called "indigenous." There are about 200 indigenous tribes, each with their own language and spiritual traditions, healing and customs. They exist by fishing, hunting and living by whatever the forest provides for them.

Most indigenous tribes have good craftsmen, such as weavers and carvers, who make dugout canoes, baskets, pottery, hunting tools and other necessary items which form the production base of their communities. They do not use a monetary system; rather, they barter for other goods such as clothing, knives, hunting and fishing tools, dry fish and fresh fruits. Some of the traded items they keep for themselves, but most are traded again for additional supplies with people who travel up and down the river communities. Indigenous people dress in skirts made of palm fibre and use vegetable dyes for textile and facial ornamental decorations.

The river is very important to the lives of the indigenous people. They use the river for washing clothes, bathing, and fishing and for cooking water. Since there are no roads in the rainforest, the rivers are their main means of transportation to get places, to maintain their social networking with other tribes and to reach their spiritual healers in case of illness. Adults and children travel by dugout canoes that are handmade from very large hardwood trees.

Constantine Issighos　　　　The Amazon Exploration Series

AMAZONIAN TARANTULAS

GIANT TARANTULAS AND CENIPEDES

The Amazon Exploration Series   Constantine Issighos

GIANT TARANTULAS AND CENIPEDES   12

GIANT TARANTULAS AND CENIPEDES

The Amazon Exploration Series — Constantine Issighos

GIANT TARANTULAS AND CENIPEDES

Constantine Issighos		The Amazon Exploration Series

15		GIANT TARANTULAS AND CENIPEDES

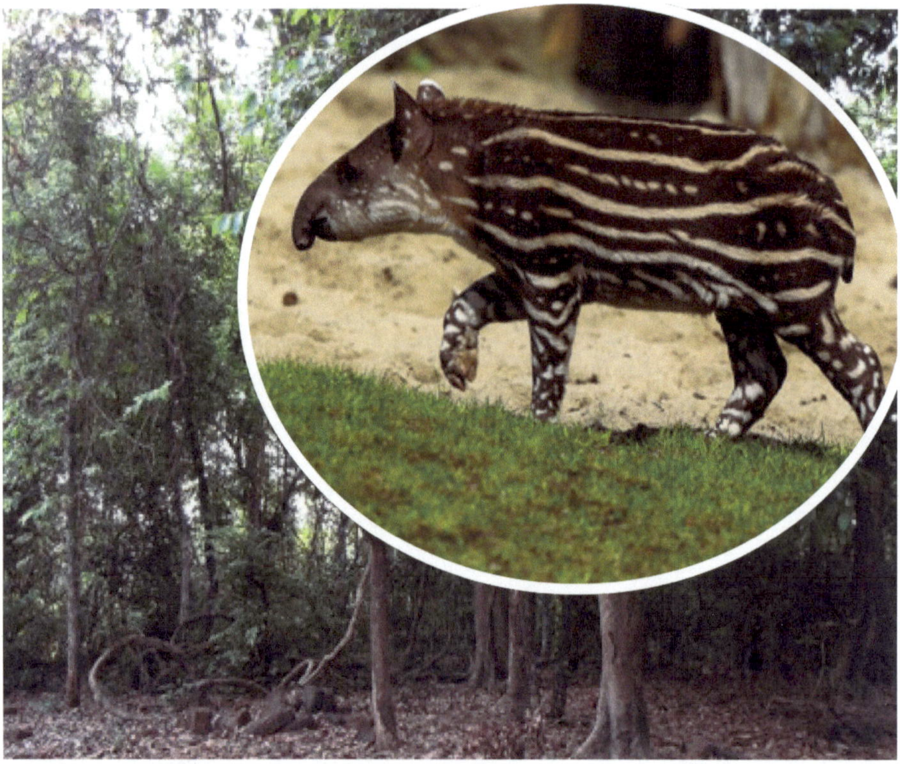

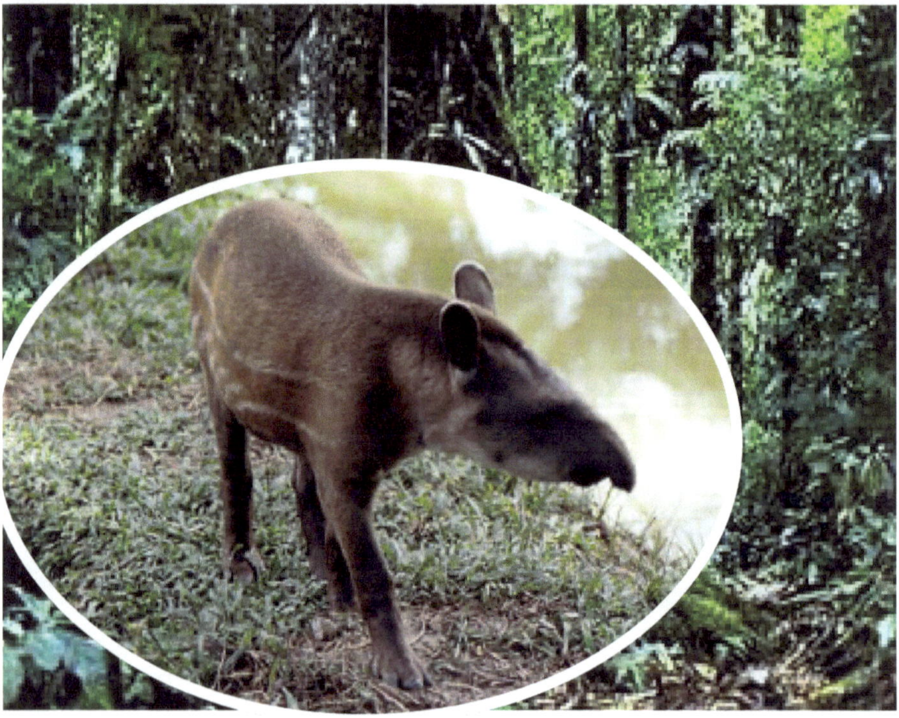

Constantine Issighos   The Amazon Exploration Series

GIANT TARANTULAS AND CENIPEDES

The Amazon Exploration Series   Constantine Issighos

GIANT TARANTULAS AND CENIPEDES   18

Constantine Issighos The Amazon Exploration Series

AMAZONIAN CENTIPEDE

GIANT TARANTULAS AND CENIPEDES

The Amazon Exploration Series — Constantine Issighos

GIANT TARANTULAS AND CENIPEDES

Constantine Issighos The Amazon Exploration Series

21 GIANT TARANTULAS AND CENIPEDES

The Amazon Exploration Series — Constantine Issighos

GIANT TARANTULAS AND CENIPEDES

The Amazon Exploration Series — Constantine Issighos

GIANT TARANTULAS AND CENIPEDES — 24

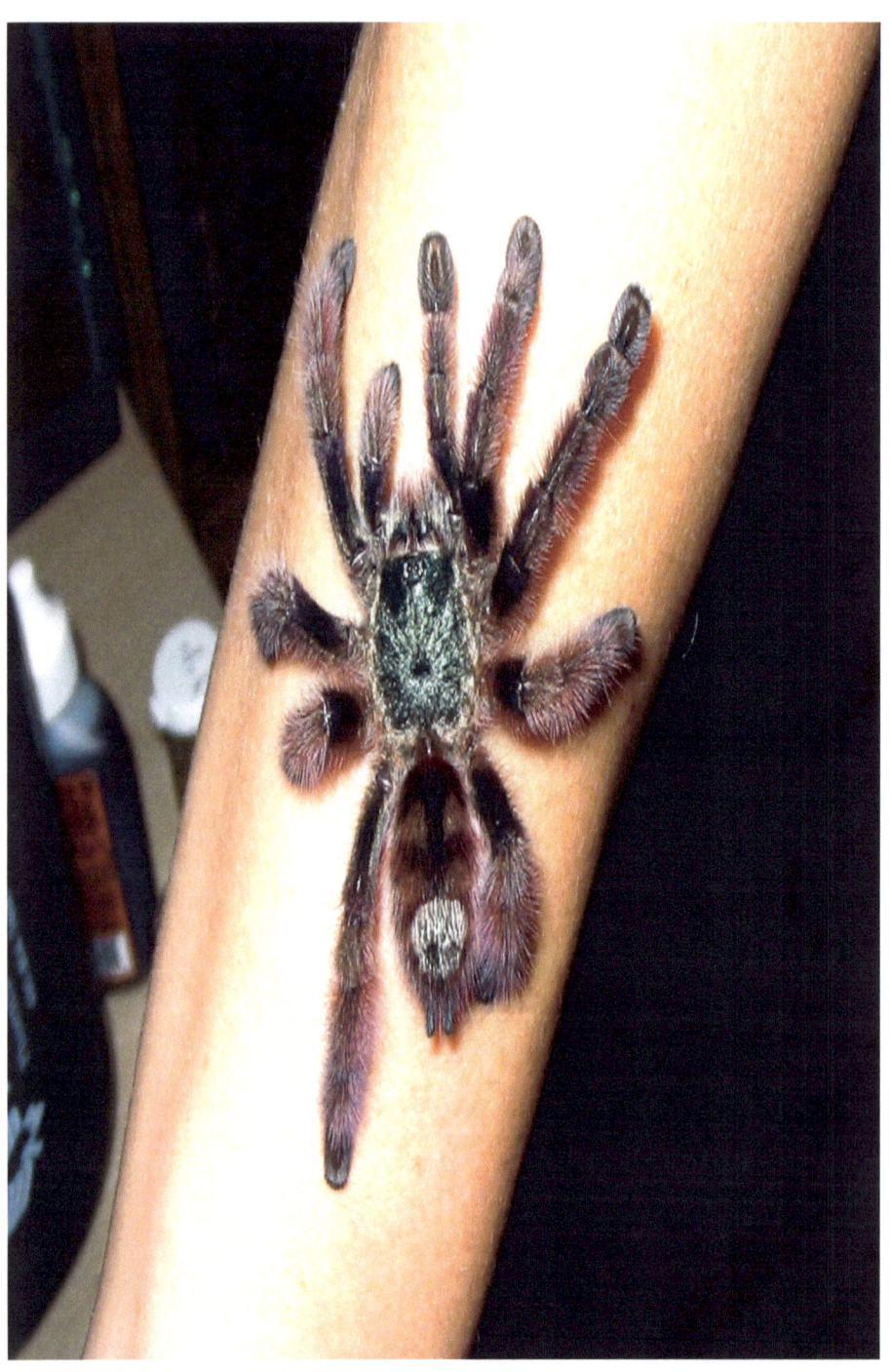

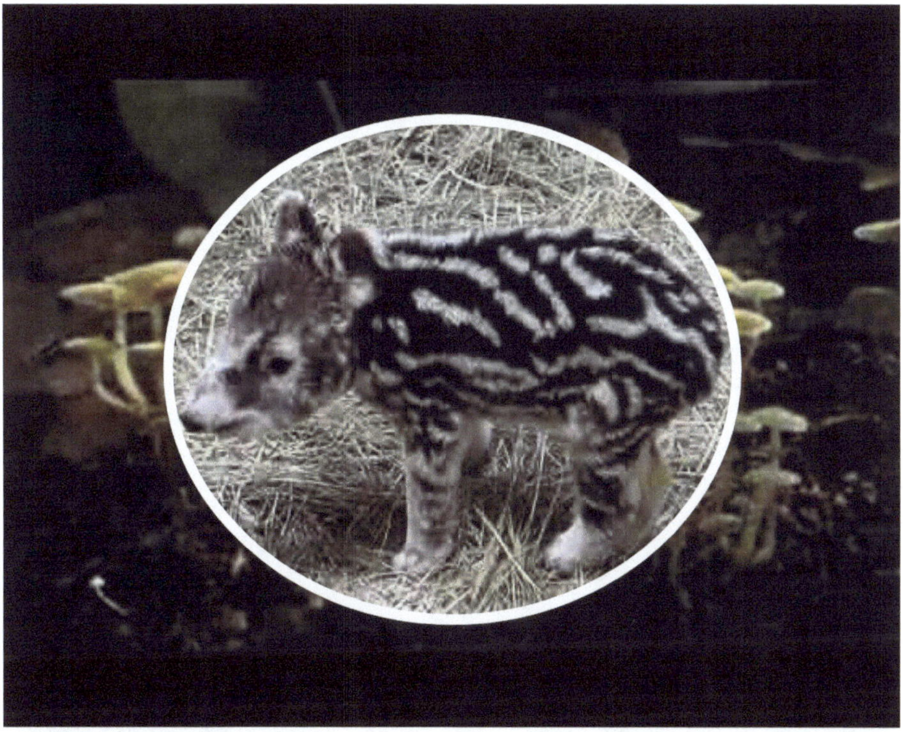

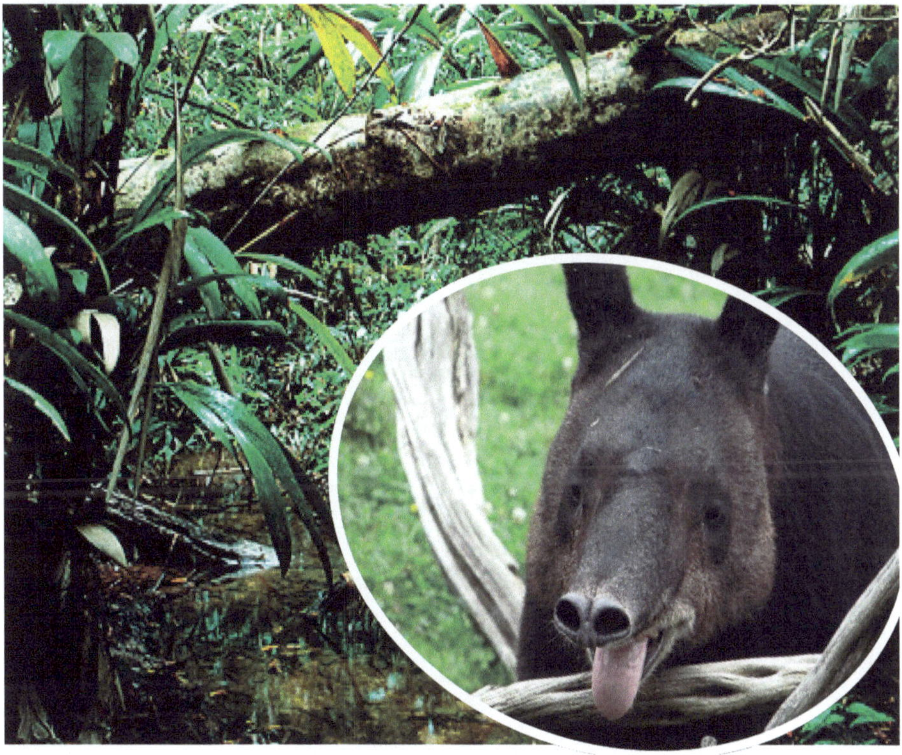

Constantine Issighos   The Amazon Exploration Series

GIANT TARANTULAS AND CENIPEDES

The Amazon Exploration Series — Constantine Issighos

GIANT TARANTULAS AND CENIPEDES

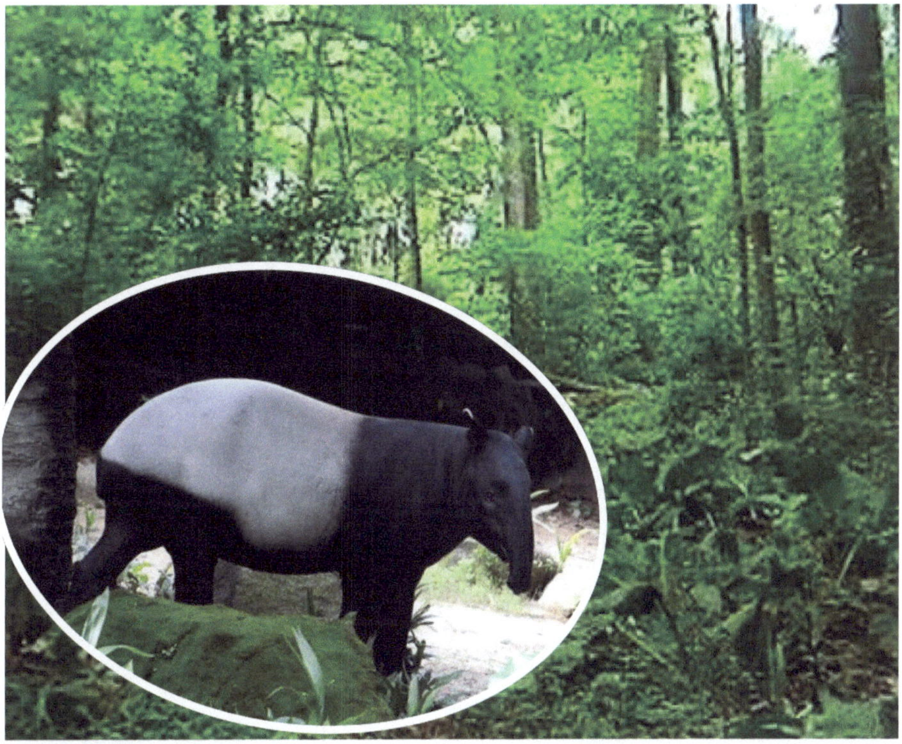

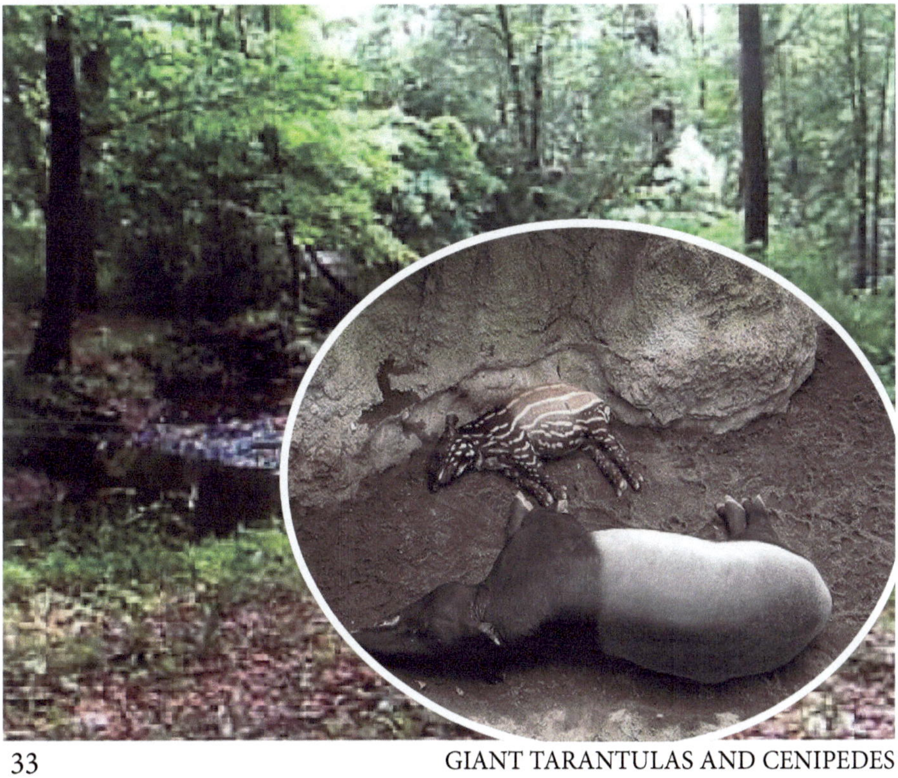

The Amazon Exploration Series   Constantine Issighos

GIANT TARANTULAS AND CENIPEDES

Constantine Issighos　　　　　The Amazon Exploration Series

35　　　　　　　　　　GIANT TARANTULAS AND CENIPEDES

Constantine Issighos   The Amazon Exploration Series

GIANT TARANTULAS AND CENIPEDES

The Amazon Exploration Series — Constantine Issighos

GIANT TARANTULAS AND CENIPEDES

The Amazon Exploration Series — Constantine Issighos

GIANT TARANTULAS AND CENIPEDES

GIANT TARANTULAS AND CENIPEDES

www.ingramcontent.com/pod-product-compliance
Lightning Source LLC
Chambersburg PA
CBHW041753040426
42446CB00001B/22